THANK YOU BECAUSE

YGAF

You Gave A Fuck!

Jason Fyk- Founder and Owner of WTF Magazine

Jennifer James- Chief Operating Officer of WTF Magazine

Jem Hologram- Editor and Content Manager of WTF Magazine

Bill Stevenson- Thank you for the inspiration to start writing.

Kelly "Dopey" Jones- Thank you for your unwavering friendship and support

David Hildick- Ditto above except Kelly's ass looks nicer in a bikini ;)

Mark Unruh- Always has a pearl of wisdom right when I need it.

Edward "Buzz Cut" Yates, Jr.- You always laughed at these stories and didn't fuck up my hair!

Melissa Caulder- Thank you for pushing me to my writing limits.

More Friends to Thank (I have the best)

Sam and Pam Chorlton

Tina Cubeta

Jennifer Olds

Susan Kalet

David and Donna O'Brien

Allisyn Ruggieri

Lori and Patrick Walsh

And most importantly………..my family!

To those I forgot to thank, SORRRY! I am incredibly WASTED!

Forward

Some serious shit before the funny shit:

I abhor political correctness and this book is an expression of my disdain for people who cannot handle words like "Fuck" and "Pussy". So….fuck you, you pussies! Stop being such thin-skinned panty-waists and concern yourself more with the real problems in the world rather than if someone tells an off-color joke or uses a word you find offensive! "Oh my, he said FUCK!" Fuck yeah…… I did☺

This book is written as the stories came out of my mouth. Once you say something, you do not have the chance to go back and edit what has already been spoken. I treated this book the same way. Grammatical errors? Yep. Punctuation fuck ups? Yep. The way this book was written is probably by some standards, as raw as the stories inside. I value substance over style. To all those teachers who would mark down a letter grade for missing a comma now and again: FUUUUCK YOU!! LOL

Reaching a point where you truly don't give a fuck anymore is liberating. Not giving a fuck doesn't

mean that you walk around blatantly trying to offend people just to be an ass hat. It also does not mean that you stop caring about ANYTHING. To me it means to be completely fearless about who you are and not concerning yourself with those who can't handle the person you are.

If the person you are drops the occasional "F-bomb", **BE** that person. If you want a tattoo, get that tat! If the people around you discourage your dreams or make fun of your goals, <u>find new friends.</u>

When I was close to finishing this book and let the word out about how raunchy it is, I was attacked. "Why would you write about your sex life???!!! "What will your children think!!??" So-called friends dropped off of my FB page. Take chances on your dreams and you find out very quickly who your real friends are. It was not all bad though. Some people who you never realized thought highly of you, will come out of the woodwork with words of encouragement.

 So why would I write this kind of book? Because I can. What will my children think? They will

always know that they have a father who loves them and they are the center of his universe. They will see a father who has the courage to live his dreams in spite of negativity surrounding him. Hopefully, they will get off of their asses earlier in life than I did and chase their dreams. If they fall down in the process, they can have a one minute pity party and start again.

Am I what my parents envisioned? LOL! Probably not since I was supposed to be a preacher! ☺
But………..

I have discovered that if you constantly try to form to a mold of who others think you should be, you will never know *who* it is….. you really are. -- Gregg

The Birth of Gregg Beerpussy

I had three dreams in my life since I was four years old: earn my black belt, play in a rock band, and become an FBI agent. The black belt was achieved, but the rock band fucked any possible hope of an FBI career! I started taking guitar lessons at age fifteen. I took lessons on and off for a while, but was not *seriously* dedicated to the instrument. I was in love with the "idea" of becoming a rock star. Look cool, live fast and play hard! It seemed interesting and a big deal, so it got the reaction and attention from people I was looking for. The truth is that I only learned enough to get by and for a very good reason… I needed to learn just enough to get laid!

Writing song lyrics took no effort for me and I found it easy to put the time and attention into it. Writing poems and song lyrics took my mind off of things like a fucked up home life. If an

ADD diagnosis existed when I was a child, I would have been the FIRST one on meds! Instead of teachers or my parents picking up on the fact that I daydreamed because I was so fucking bored and needed to be truly challenged, I was called a lazy piece of shit.

I was definitely a dreamer, **no doubt**. Instead of being encouraged to live my dreams, I was consistently told that things were unrealistic, impossible, or just outright stupid ideas. My asshole brother would relentlessly torment me by following me around singing the Supertramp song *"Dreamer/ you're nothing but a dreamer / Dreamer/ you're nothing but a dreamer*!" Teasing….. Non-fucking-stop. I had a phone conversation with him recently and he brought that up. He said: "Remember how I used to tease you with that song Dreamer?" NOOOOO… why would I remember that?? WTF?! Asshole. He said, "You have actually accomplished two out of the three. Too bad the FBI thing won't work out." Yeah, fuck you bro. In the words of Meatloaf, "Two out of three ain't bad." Long live Mr. Meat, the meatiest, the mad meatster….

So, I would take my occasional lessons and have pictures taken of me posing with my guitar. I was in love with the image. The **idea** of being a star and surrounded by the hot, sexed up women who would flash their tits and drop to their knees just to honk on Bobo was a huge draw for this boy! My shorts get tight just thinking about it! Sorry teacher, I cannot come to the blackboard. I will take the zero ;)

I played sports but I wasn't a stand out athlete. I received great scores on standardized tests, but was not scoring with the girls. I always seemed to take off like a rocket on things I tried, but fizzled out very quickly. *That was not an "in-the-sack" reference*, you sick bastards! No fizzling out in the sack for me. I take longer to launch than the fucking space shuttle Challenger.

The thing that never faded was my desire to be noticed. Often times, just being noticed for being different or crazy was at least _something_. It was a classic case of middle child syndrome. I was constantly pounded (not from behind, you sick fucks) with questions about why I wasn't "Applying myself". At this point, I am not going too deep into the reasons for this because I want to write more about the crazy and fun side of things but I will get into the darker, interpersonal side that

helped foster my need for attention in another book someday. Only a brave step into therapy gave me the insight into how and why my brain is as fucked up as it is.

With all of the excesses I indulged in, I am lucky to be alive. My attitude is similar to something I heard Keith Richards say at a concert. He was about to play one of the few songs he sings lead on and looked out at the crowd while they clapped with a huge smile on his face. Smiling he said: "Thank you, I am glad to be here." He chuckled and then added: "Matter of fact, I'm glad to be anywhere!" The crowd got it and laughed hysterically.

So……. all that I wanted to do was be on stage, party, and most of all: RELENTLESSLY BANG AS MANY WILLING WOMEN AS I COULD! I was the guy who, in middle and high school, was every girl's "best friend." While my other friends were busy "sealing the deal," I was listening to the girls tell me their problems and why guys are such assholes. I might as well have been the "gay friend." Damn, suck one dick and you're a homo for life! Kidding……. too salty for me. The sight of someone else's balls…….no thanks. Ladies who like the balls: while I enjoy that you to treat them nicely, I don't get the

attraction. But please……be kind to Ping and Pong. They are nice fellows down below ☺ Just a couple of nuts with an asshole and real dick for next door neighbors.

The wild sex-capades and rock-star dreams played equal roles during my teens and twenties. My family moved to a new area when I was twelve years old. An insanely fun family lived next door. Italian mother and crazy Irish father - a wicked brew. Whereas my parents were very conservative Christians, we would hear rock music and cursing blasting out of their house at equal volume. I wasn't even allowed to *listen* to rock music, let alone utter a single, "Motherfucker!" My mother once came into my room like a wild-eyed banshee one night screaming, *"TURN OFF THAT SATAN'S EVIL ROCK AND ROLL!!!"* It was fucking *George Thorogood* for Christ's sake! Anyway… Good thing they never found out about the plants I used to start on the garage roof. Shit! I guess they know now!

There were four kids in the family next door: the two oldest were girls, the younger two boys. The girls loved to sit and talk to me. They

took pleasure in corrupting me with Satan's evil rock albums. Hail to the fucking Prince of Darkness! They introduced me to Aerosmith, The Stones, Boston and eventually The Ramones. The list could go on forever. The oldest girl was also responsible for my earliest legitimate sexual training. As I said, sex and rock n' roll were forever bonded together in my brain. One did not exist without the other. My time spent with her forever sealed that bond like Krazy Glue. Sex took my attention away from spending my time on the actual hard work that goes into making music. At least I don't look back with regret that I passed up too many opportunities!

    I soon happily learned that my girl next door was more of a **nympho next door.** At this point I should mention that I was twelve and she was nearing seventeen. I was barely in middle school, and she was nearing the end of high school. I loved the attention! She had big tits with eraser sized nipples for Christ' sake! They were things I had only really seen in a *Hustler* magazine that a construction worker had left behind when our house was built.

We took a break from listening to records one day to go for a walk. There wasn't much else to do in our semi-rural neighborhood. I lived in an area that was surrounded by some very beautiful woods. The woods could tell their own stories. It is amazing how something as simple as a group of trees could hold so many memories. We would tear through those woods on our dirt bikes in search of the best place to stop for a toke. There was some "Getting wood in the woods" on the day "Kathleen" and I took that walk. Random question that I ponder: If you took a cross section of a wiener, could you count the rings to tell how many times someone got laid? Hmmmmm…I will leave that for the autopsy folks. Note to my future mortitian: Please make sure my crotch is pitching a tent while I lie in the coffin just to fuck with people. If I am going to be referred to as a stiff, I at least want to be……stiff. Add some size for good measure too….thank you in advance.

A few years later, in almost the exact spot where we made out, another neighbor girl and I laid down and went down on each other until we added our own dew to the ground. In those days,

you went down until your jaw ached and you blew out a few taste buds from the furious pussy buffet once you found her clit! It felt good and you were just fucking happy to be doing it.

From what I remember, I don't think I had any intent on actually hooking up or having any kind of sexual relationship with the girl next door. I am sure that I beat my meat like it owed me money thinking about it, but I had no actual serious thought of anything happening.

We did our normal walking and talking, and I can't remember any of the content of our conversation. Whatever we talked about was probably erased from my memory bank by the events that unfolded next. We took a few steps into the woods when my nympho neighbor stopped and posed a question. She asked, "Do you mind if I give you kissing lessons?" *Do I mind*?????? *Are you fucking kidding*?????? I am not sure how quickly I agreed to those "lessons," but it was probably faster than any theory Einstein or Larry Flynt could have come up with! What followed was the first of many intertwining of tongues and

make-out sessions that should have bloodied our lips.

Her tutoring was **top-notch**! She taught me how to use my lips and tongue in just the right way: Sensual but not careless and clumsy like some dumb jock getting his first piece of ass. There were many more lessons and kissing became a familiar routine. Eventually things went to another level.

I had left the on-deck circle and was ready for a legit at-bat. Major League baby! One day we were listening to albums in her room. Since we had such an age difference, I don't think it ever registered with her parents that anything worthy of supervision could be going on upstairs. During a kissing lesson to the soundtrack of the first Boston album, she asked me if I would like to touch her boobs. She may have said go to second base, I don't fucking remember! What I remember was her practically soaking her panties just from me furiously rubbing her massive "Dirty pillows!" She was telling ME to keep the noise down but HER moans and breathing were the things that could have gotten us caught!! "Be careful, you are

moving on the bed too much," she said. Ha!! She was the one that needed to put a lid on things! *Besides, we could have just moved to the floor....or stood up...or in hindsight..... from behind.....even better!*

One interesting thing about an older girl who wants to give a young boy kissing lessons is that she knows OTHER older girls who want to give younger boys kissing lessons! Apparently, she confided in a girlfriend about what we had been up to. Eventually I was making out and reaching second base with her freak of a friend too. They were sharing and I was a happy boy! I was truly a kid in a candy store of carnal delight. There was no way my friends could understand THIS shit! I would tell my friends the stories and they would listen with mouths wide open like I was reading stories from the old Penthouse Forum. Whenever her friend came over, I got to move between the two engaging in marathon French kissing and tit groping.

I never thought for a second that anything was fucked up about the shit going on even though there was a major gap in age. Some have suggested

otherwise. The reality is that the volcano in my gonads started long before these two came along! They merely started the flow of MOLTEN GONAD LAVA. I was more than a willing participant!

Things reached a point with her friend where I encountered a dilemma. *What happens when you start having romantic feelings for someone when their only intent was a purely physical relationship?* THAT is a complicated decision for a twelve year old.

For some reason, I never thought of the girl next door as anything other than a friend. We shared a relationship based on music and sex. No feelings of romance or any boyfriend/girlfriend stuff. We were the original "Friends with benefits." Her friend…… was a different story.

I definitely started to feel like she was my girlfriend, or at least I *wanted* her to be. I was FLOORED when I saw her get into a car with Kathleen's cousin to go out on a date. My jaw was on the ground, heart in my throat and I wanted to throw up. I am positive he was pounding that

sloppy snatch by the end of the night. It broke my heart. I am not sure why I had feelings for Kathleen's friend. I cannot remember if she led me in that direction or if I just went there on my own. What matters is that I fell - and **fell hard**. Maybe I started to believe that a twelve year old boy could actually have a seventeen year old girlfriend.

    We did eventually have a discussion where she explained to me that her only interest was to have a little fun. I think my neighbor felt badly about bringing her friend into our "Kissing class" and encouraged her to have THAT talk. It was the kind of conversation where you look like you are listening, but all you hear is that garbled "Wha Wha Wha Wha" sound like the teacher from the Charlie Brown cartoons in your skull.

    That whole deal really fucked with my head! At that time of my life I had no understanding of relationships or how healthy ones develop. I guess I thought that if someone went so far as to let you venture into their panties, naturally a relationship could follow. Go figure!

Eventually, all of the lessons in fun with flesh went by the wayside and everyone moved on. Other than messing around a little with the girls in my church youth group at the Christian school I went to, **(Hint: preacher's daughters are some of the biggest freaks on the planet!)** I was not past third base for a while. When I was sixteen a wonderful girl changed all of that.

I remember I was so concerned with being a good lover the day I lost my cherry, I watched the clock on her night stand so that I could make sure I lasted a respectable length of time. The funniest shit is what I said to a friend of mine when I got back from her house: "Man it was fucking awesome!! I am never whacking off again! LOL BIG…..LIE!!!!

Men, here is a dose of Beerpussy wisdom from my early experience: **Always, always, always get your girl off first!!** After she gets off, you are on your way to stardom. If you can make her come again, you are in the same category as a CD gone Platinum! If you become a true master, you might just achieve the stratosphere of sex mastery known as LEVEL BEERPUSSY.

The rock n' roll education I got from Kathleen was beyond words. She was always playing records for me and she was so enthusiastic every time she found a new artist. What she did not realize is that she had stumbled upon a recipe. It was a recipe for something new and more dangerous than nitroglycerin in the hands of an epileptic:

Gregg Beerpussy

-2 cups sex fiend

-1 cup party animal

- Just a dash of real musician

But there was something missing…………

Sealing the deal was still a bit of a challenge, but I was very observant and a quick learner. I got to watch one of the best when I worked at the beach after my senior year of high school.

Toby was one of the ugliest fucking dudes I have ever met. He had a pock marked face and

fucked up teeth that would put Austin Powers to shame, but he thought he was **KING SHIT**.

This asshole would literally stand in the mirror while drying his hair bragging about what a good-looking motherfucker he was! He carried his lacrosse stick on the boardwalk (WTF?) and wore a jersey with the number "69" on it. Yes….. he did. Funny thing about that douche bag Toby, he got more ass than any of the other guys I worked with! He was getting some fairly quality tail too and these girls had all holes open for business.

Some of these girls weren't the brightest……….but …….it *was* **pussy**, and certainly more than I was getting. I just didn't like how Toby treated girls like shit after he got his rocks off. Mommy issues, I guess. Watching Toby *did* expose the missing ingredient for the final recipe for **Gregg Beerpussy Stew**:

-2 cups sex fiend

-1 cup party animal

-3 cups of attitude

-2 cups of naturally occurring nice guy

-And that splash of real musician

Mix the ingredients thoroughly, turn the oven on high, and it is feeding time at the Rock n' Roll Porno Zoo!

Enjoy your meal folks because you are about to get a mouthful of Gregg Beerpussy Surprise! Spit or swallow, the choice is yours………

THERE IS NO PUSSY…..

LIKE BEERPUSSY!!

"Some mornings you wake up and feel like a horse just STOMPED on your head and FUCKED you in the eye!"-Unknown

Hi, my name is Gregg Beerpussy. You are probably thinking: "Yeah right, *your* name is Gregg Beerpussy. That is **too cool** of a name for *anyone* to actually have." Okay, you are right. It is not my real name. If you did really stop for **even a second** and have that thought, you have killed way more brain cells than I and need to stop licking toads, eating 'shrooms or whatever the fuck it is you are doing! You will DEFINITELY appreciate this book's celebration of juvenile behavior run wild.

"**Beerpussy**" is more of a statement to the mentality of my days spent working with, and playing in, rock bands. Everyone in this story that played in the band will bear the last name Beerpussy because they too shared the same state of mind. The drummer from our band will be the only one not **honored** with the last name Beerpussy. For the purpose of this story, his last

name will be **"Nuttbutter."** You will find out the reason for that later.

It mainly has to do with the fact that he is, and always will be, the equivalent of douche waste. I *am* thankful that Tommy introduced me to the young lady that is part of the story behind **"Nut butter,"** but other than that he was just a douche.

"Beerpussy" is actually the shortened version of choices for last names that would accurately describe our exploits, because **"Beerpussyassholemouthwithmultiplepartnersoccasionaldruguse"** was a bit too much to type over and over.

Of course, one of the real reason people change names is to protect people's identities (in this case, the INSANELY GUILTY). An ex has heard the majority of the stories and for some reason still hangs out with me. The woman has never watched porn and one night uttered the words **"Oh my God you are huge!"** She had me at "Huge!" Some say the way to a man's heart is

through his stomach. **Fuck that**! Compliment his cock.

All adult programming in our home was **blocked,** and I will forever remain THE biggest cock until she finds one bigger. What I am saying is that I, Gregg Beerpussy, don't feel any potential backlash from sharing my stories**. If** any issues do come up I just hope this book makes enough money so I can go back to my days as a proud man-whore!

If you paid to read this book, **THANK YOU!!!** It might mean more MILF for me this time around. Yes, I said **MORE** MILF. We were hitting MILF in 1984 well before it became an actual term and porn category. The difference is the "**I'd like to**" part. For us it would be "**Moms Unashamedly Fucked Fantastically" (MUFF)**

Our bass player, **Sid Beerpussy**, also shares my lack of fear or shame about these stories seeing the light of day. If I recall correctly his words were: "**as long as the story is about me ass-slamming some hot chick, go the fuck ahead**!" Mick Beerpussy *might* be another story and

obviously I don't give a fuck about Tommy Nuttbutter.

It is not my problem if anyone is ashamed of their past. To me, your past is always part of your present. It is a major part of who you are. Due to my past exploits I have been able to show one of my exes tricks she had never experienced. One move she especially liked is what I call the "Lick and Stick." To perform it properly, you slide a dildo inside her while lapping at her clit. It is almost a guaranteed orgasmic payday!

Today I, **Gregg Beerpussy,** would appear to the casual observer as a responsible father who is living the suburban dream. If one were able to play back my brain like a movie and view the trail of carnal delight, they would either **vomit**, run to their therapist, act like a jealous asshole or **jerk off**. With some, all of those things might happen simultaneously!

There were people that actually HATED us for how much action we got! Mick and I worked for a band, and their bass player could not comprehend our exploits. He said we were making

shit up, etc... Well……. just like Tommy Nuttbutter……..he eventually received his lesson in the power of Gregg Beerpussy. I was regularly bringing pleasure to one of his former girlfriends as only a man named Beerpussy could do! Even after we broke up, she asked me if we could still get together and fuck! I love my life ☺ Who says nice guys finish last? Whoever it is tell them to shut the fuck up! Ah, if only all break-ups could go that way….It turns out that he claimed to have fucked her regularly and…..he NEVER did. She laughed out loud when she heard his claims! **If you don't have game, don't make the claim dude!!!** Ha! Amateur! Don't fuck with me mortal!

    I never did become a rich or famous rock star. Looking back now, I realize that I **did** actually live my rock n' roll fantasy: CONSTANT partying, A LOT of sex, booze, drugs and oh yeah, the playing music part! I was broke as hell, lived in a shitty apartment with three asshole roommates, drove a car that only ran occasionally, but I was racking up pussy points faster than a porn star on crack. Mick used to say that it never mattered **what** kind of car I drove. The confidence

in my ability to trap beaver could overcome **ANYTHING**.

Merely saying you play in a band **AND** looking the part got you action. **If you actually had a tape** (I am old) to play for a girl, HOLY SHIT! You could forget about unzipping your pants because she would usually be doing the work **FOR YOU** about 1:30 into the second song! She spent the first song *debating* if unzipping your pants would make her seem slutty. No, of course not! Don't be silly…..

I recently helped with security at a major rock festival. A very lovely girl in her early 20's was BEGGING me to let her back stage. This girl was a natural beauty. She had long straight brown hair, no makeup and a beautiful tan. Her look was the definition of girl next door. My shorts are getting tight and I am wishing she was the **"Girl that lived next door to _me_!"** So…..this young

lady was offering herself up to me because she wanted to get backstage and meet the 50 something lead singer of The Red Hot Chili Peppers. Her words to me will ring on forever among the things I hope **NEVER** to hear from my daughter: **"If he fucks me just once I know he will love me."** FUCK x ONCE does not = LOVE. Sorry babe, should have paid attention in math class.

    That exchange really brought into focus what fueled her desire. It is pure rock n' roll! Well that and probably daddy issues…..just a guess. Not having money, or having never made the big time did not diminish the ability to get as much tail as I wanted, do as many drugs as I could and **drink my face off.** One of the other perks is that my insane antics were EXPECTED.

 I heard a recent statistic that claimed a man's chances of dipping his wick go up 17% just by carrying a guitar. I can only imagine what the statistics are if you can **actually play the fucking thing!**

    Of course, if you are a broke musician, you may not be on a private jet or yacht while you are taking the "Tongue boat to tuna town." The action

may occur in a club bathroom or a band truck. **Who really gives a shit?!!!** Your conquest may not *look* like a supermodel, but so what?! Some of the hottest girls I ever came across in my band days could not fuck their way out of a paper bag.

For some reason, certain girls think that if they **look** good, they can get away with just lying there with arms and legs spread out like a starfish. Gee, don't break a sweat or anything!! Once you get used to the reality that you are **constantly** getting laid, looks are **not** good enough. **BRING ME SOME TALENT!!!**

People might read this book and think that I spent my time preying on innocent young women. WRONG! First, they were not *always*………. young ;)) Secondly, we **NEVER** misled anyone when it came to our intentions. Frequently we weren't the ones with the heat-seeking meat! We didn't need to get girls drunk or make up shitty lines to get into their pants. More often than not, those pants came off all……. by……themselves! Sometimes **my** *own* **clothes** came off without lifting a finger!

Merely being **in** the rock scene gets you laid. Sometimes being a roadie, sound man, or working the lights was an **even better** position to be in. The ability to scope the crowd and just pick that low hanging poontang fruit was *too* easy at times. There are at least a few stories in this book that came from just being "With the band".

Recently my ex and I were discussing some of my many exploits and she said in an almost impressed tone: "Damn, you got a lot of tail!" **Yes, dear, I did!** If you ran a calculation of the average number of sexual partners a person has had and multiplied that by the number of women I have had sex with, you have been sleeping with over at least seven hundred people worth of experience! The test I took in my life I am most proud of passing was my HIV test. For some reason my stories don't seem to scare her - but then again, she **always** made me wear a rubber. LOL!

Enjoy the "tales of tail" in this book. Laugh if you want, shake your head; say to yourself, "These things can't be true!" I read them myself, look at my dick and say, "Glad you're still with me buddy!" You have my word that every story in

this book happened. Hey, if you can't trust a guy named "Beerpussy" who can you trust?

As I said to an ex as we were having sex for the first time: **"JUST YOU WAIT, THIS IS ONLY THE TIP!"**

Life's a Beach

"It's not gay if it's in a three-way"- Lonely Island

"It's not gay if it's in a MANY person way"- Gregg Beerpussy

Share and share alike! Almost always we were willing to share girls. There were only a **few** we were selfish about sharing with each other. On occasion a few of them were shared……..I assure you…….. PURELY by accident! But… more to come on that later. Or do I mean more come will come? Or someone will come on someone? **DAMMIT I AM CONFUSED!** It is the alcohol talking, I swear!

Anyway….. The sharing wasn't **always** full-on sex with each other's partners - I will call them….. "Group activities." Some stuff was relatively tame late-night naked pillow fights running through hotels with our female guests or streaking across a college campus with a group of adventurous girls. There were other nights though that we cranked things up to **FULL BEERPUSSY** and "Our amps went to 11!" Long live Spinal Tap!

One particular evening stands out for a whole shit-ton of reasons. The night started off in its' usual way. We played our music and drank unbelievable amounts of alcohol.

 In between the second and third set, a twenty-one year old sweetheart **AND her hot mom** (who was sporting a **nice** set of fake tits) invited me back to their place after the gig so that I could fuck them both! It was the daughter's birthday. The mother was going to let the birthday girl blow my veined flesh candle and then mom promised to "**destroy**" me after I finished off the daughter! Fucked up family dynamics? Maybe, but who am I to judge???!! It was a Jerry Springer wet dream**.**

Oh my fucking God, why did I pick the wrong time to have a girlfriend with me?!?! As messed up as the whole situation may (or may not) sound, this would have been a good story to put in the book for sure! But… I **had** to decline. We were at the beach, hours from home, so it wasn't realistic to send the girlfriend packing. Taking advantage of this opportunity would have probably caused me to wind up on some "Who's the daddy?" episode of Maury. Girlfriend or not, I was at the beach,

rocking out, drunk and horny. **Go ahead…. hate me for being a slut and considering it!**

I am more disappointed that I didn't try to work my girlfriend in on the action! I was drunk and for once not thinking on my feet. I am disappointed that for the only time in history, my dick wasn't doing the thinking!!! Damn, you fucktard of a flesh torpedo!! **YOU HAVE FAILED ME!!!**

This night things probably got more out of control than usual because Sid, his girl, my girl and I were crashing in the apartment over the club. No one had to drive anywhere so it was definitely "Game on!" and you NEVER knew what to expect with us. To say there were NO LIMITS is an understatement. We were a bunch of depraved lunatics and took pride in it!

Mick and Sid were hanging out at the bar downing shots and beer after the gig alongside some customers finishing their last drinks. Standing next to Sid at the bar was some redneck guy (just assuming based on the flannel shirt…. cammo hat….missing teeth….etc.), eyeing him up like the punk rock oddity he was. After Mick and Sid

downed a shot, Sid immediately realized he was going to hurl. He grabbed his large empty beer glass, chucked, and filled it to the rim with puke as the redneck with fishing lures on his hat looked on in horror.

 Without missing a beat, Sid placed the puke filled glass on the bar and slid it in front of the redneck dude as he pointed and with a wink said: **"Hey pal, this one's on me!"** Yet another classic Sid one liner. I thought for sure this was going to result in an ass whipping for Sid, but I think that poor motherfucker's mind was so scrambled by Sid that he had no come back. The outrageous **fuckery** continued when we went upstairs to the apartment after the gear was loaded out and the bar closed.

	Sid's girlfriend at the time was always cold to me. The girl seemed to **hate my guts**. SID WAS AS FUCKED UP IN THE HEAD, or more, than I was! I am not sure where her attitude came from, but whatever. This night she was a little nicer.

 As we were hanging out in the living room of the apartment, Sid decided to break out his girlfriend's camera. He handed it to me and said to start taking

some pictures of "Marilyn." As my girlfriend looked on, Sid gave Marilyn instructions on what to do, **and man did she enjoy it**! I am not sure if it was because she had some "never going to hit this" tease mentality going on toward me or what but hey, WHO THE FUCK CARES?!!!! I was photographing pussy. I was POONANY PAPPARAZI! Life was good! Sid guided her through the photo session like a pro. He should have gone into porn. A move he pulled on Marilyn later would convince me of that.

 After the photo shoot, Sid and Marilyn started going at it full-throttle, legs behind the ears pile driving with more force than hydraulic fracking! It was at that point I witnessed something I had NEVER seen before. I will call it, "The shoot, re-load and fire again, semen squirt." My guy Sid pulled out, spewed his man jam on her and then re-entered to continue his full on sex commando snapper assault until he managed to launch another spew of pecker-snot all over her chest. I just stared in pure admiration. The man was an animal. See, he should have gone into porn!

Turnabout is fair play so I let him "pose" my girlfriend's love-folds for some classic shots. On that night, I definitely could not go toe to toe, or gonad to gonad with Sid and his "move." I did my best, which fortunately was enough for my girl. After all of the action, everyone was starving. Here is where a relatively tame incident happened that got us banned from the apartment AND any future gigs at this particular bar.

The pizza was the last thing to come in the apartment that night. The girls and I were eating pizza on the couch but Sid was squatting naked in the middle of the room, with his semi-automatic super schlong dangling inches from the pizza while chowing on his slice. The owner of the bar and apartment walked in on this scene and his jaw HIT THE FUCKING FLOOR! Sid just looked at him blankly, and with a slight head bob said: "Hey, what's up man? Thanks for letting us crash here!" The dude was speechless. Nudity, cameras and the sight of Sid squatting over a pepperoni pie! It was more than this poor bastard's brain could handle. He grabbed whatever he came for and walked out without saying a word.

We found out later that the owner approached Mick the next morning while we were all loading out our gear and asked: "What the FUCK is wrong with your band???!!" He then recounted the scene to Mick and Mick was more than a little pissed. We weren't asked back. Surprise!! **Fuck that place**. The night was worth it! This attitude is probably exactly why I never made it in the rock biz.

Brown-eye Becky and The Anal Arsonist

"Anyone that says things happen for a reason has never had a candlestick break off in their ass" - Unknown

Right now I am listening to "Sir Psycho Sexy" by the Red Hot Chili Peppers. When Anthony Keidis sings "He's a freak of nature but we love him so. He's a freak of nature but we let him go", I can't help but think "Sir Psycho Sexy" would be the perfect nickname for Sid Beerpussy. Depending on where this chapter winds up in this book, his exploits speak for themselves!

I was a participant in many of the adventures BUTT not this one. Bad pun….I couldn't resist. At first I thought this story was BULLSHIT. I thought it was TOO crazy to be true. After all of the things we had done, I have no idea why I even doubted him. This entire story was confirmed years later by "Becky" herself!

Before I tell the tale it requires a proper description of the players. Sid was the prototype of a punk-rocker. He had a hair color that constantly changed and no matter what, he had that shit spiked as high as possible.

 Once we were at a redneck bar and some hillbilly bar fly asked Sid "How do ya' get yer har to stand up like that?" Sid blandly replied: "Camel sperm. No shit, I have it imported from Saudi Arabia." That **dumbass backwoods fuck** actually said "Wow, ain't that some shit!" So there is Sid's profile: short, skinny punker with hair so high "Heat Miser" would have been proud! He looked like a punk-rock version of Phyllis Diller.

Becky, oh brown eye Becky. Her ass, her ass, her ass is on fire! Actually it wasn't just her **ass,** but we will get to that part in a bit. Becky liked to be ass-slammed more than ANYTHING else. You would have thought she had her ass and vagina confused! Possibly some type of orifice dyslexia????

DON'T misunderstand, Sid, Mick and I were BIG fans of "Puffy the Wrinkled Starfish", so that is

NOT a criticism! Unfortunately, EVERY woman I have ever met who thought the anus was hole numero-uno turned out to be a little psycho. A girl that will go in that direction every now and again to mix things up is my kind of superstar.

 Just to be clear the mothers of my children have asses with a permanent "exit only" sign hanging on them! Go ahead, feel sorry for me. It's ok! My therapist is helping me come to terms with it. But I digress….

Becky had a housemate who was a huge black dude with an obvious dislike of Sid. On this night, he inflicted ABSOLUTE HORROR on him.

Ok…… here we go. Sid and Becky were out partying and went back to her place for….. you guessed it, a relentless session of touring the turd-tunnel! When they reached the bedroom she jumped on all fours immediately, waiting for Sid to penetrate her well lubed poop tube. He set about pounding her fart-flume with the tenacity of a horny leg humping Pit Bull. Both of them were so completely focused on their **butthole bonanza** that they didn't notice that they were causing her

nightstand to wobble. That does not sound like a big deal….unless there is a CANDLE on that nightstand! I kind of think you all know what is about to come! Actually, Sid never did get….. to come.

That candle fell onto Becky's pillow and set it aflame. Initially Sid didn't realize that the increased volume of her screams wasn't due to his ass mastery! Sid was drunk and just kept plowing away. The pillow was on fire, Becky was on fire and he was blissfully unaware. The screams were increasing in intensity and the HUGE black dude burst through the door yelling "WHAT THE FUCK IS GOING ON IN HERE!!!!"

Sid opened his eyes because of the yelling and in horror finally understood the anal inferno that he was dick slamming. In fear for his life and being the **true gentleman** he is, Sid grabbed his clothes and made a dash for it. He was hopping down the sidewalk trying to get his shoes on as he ran and could hear the fire whistle as he limped away, brown dick and all.

Sid recounted the story to me and I still can't believe he left her there on fire! I said something along the likes of: "I can't believe you left her there on fire!" Sid replied nonchalantly "Hey, I thought the fucking guy was going to KILL me. No sense in two of us getting hurt! Besides, I went to see her in the hospital. That counts for something, right? She said everything was cool." Only Sid could slam a girl's turd cutter, **help set her on fire** AND have everybody be cool about it! Even the roommate agreed not to kick his ass when he came over again. That's right, he was allowed back in. Back in the house, and through her back door.

Years later I was a cubicle jockey at a large bank. In the cubicle next to me was a girl I didn't know well but we would make occasional small talk. I told her I used to play in a band around town and she asked who was in it. I mentioned Sid and she said "I know Sid." She then pulled her blouse away from her neck to reveal the burn scars of none other than…….. Brown Eye Becky! I was in fear for my job because I started laughing uncontrollably. My path to Human Resources was

getting lubed faster than her ass. She then said the words that alternately made me feel shocked and at ease all at the same time. She remarked: "I heard you guys used to have a nickname for me. I like it." I confess…I got hard. Don't judge me!

Double your pleasure, double your fun

When you can have two, why settle for one?

Sex on rooftops, in bathroom stalls, one girl licking the shaft and another licking your balls. Oh, yes….the threesome fantasy. **The Holy Grail when you are a horny male**. Damn, can't stop rhyming….hold on…..deep breath……Ok, I'm cool now.

I would like to be able to tell a story of masterful" **Beerpussy Savvy"** and how I engineered this three-way, but in reality it happened with NO EFFORT at all on my part. Thank you again rock n' roll. Thank you freaky girlfriend **and thank you to the willing third party!**

Having a girlfriend while you are playing in a band can be dicey. Jealous types are **nothing** but trouble and high maintenance. You are out in bars playing in front of drunk horny women. Part of the JOB is

to make sure you give them a REASON to keep following you from gig to gig! If you have a clingy chick that wants to claim you as property while you are mingling with the crowd, it is a serious buzz kill and the relationship WILL NOT LAST. You can be **a pussy whipped fool** and quit your band or…. kick her ass to the curb.

The girlfriend in this next scenario wasn't the jealous type AND she was a total freak. Blow jobs on demand, liked it a little rough from behind with a lot of spanking AND hair pulling for good measure. Every hole was open for business AND not only was she into porn, but she would pick out the movies and bring them home! Good for the short term but, as time would tell, not for the long term. There was just TOO much shit she was willing to do! I took full advantage.

 When I sensed I might find a bunny boiling in my kitchen one day, I cut things off faster than Lorena Bobbitt. Before that, there was some pretty cool shit going down as well as being gone down on. So here is how one night, things evolved into what was an awesome **double-decker pecker wrecker**!

We were out in one of the spots where I frequently played and, on occasion, would go to hang out. It was fun to hang out in a place you play sometimes because people knew who you were. People would buy you drinks, bands would ask you to sit in…..and most of all, you were free to live it up! Living it up could go very right or sometimes VERY WRONG. One night I was getting a blowjob in the bathroom stall at this same club from an awesomely hot girl. She had jet black hair, was part Asian and had lips that constricted my member like a python. Believe it or not, this is one story where things went wrong! "HOW IS THAT POSSIBLE GREGG??" you ask. Give me a FUCKING MINUTE and I will tell you!!!

 As I am receiving this deep-throat delight I hear the bathroom door fly open and a dude yell: "WHERE THE FUCK IS MY WIFE!!!!" OOOOPS!!! By the sudden removal of my cock from her mouth, it was obvious **that I was looking at the top of his wife's head**! I am lucky she didn't clench up and lop off my member! She crouched with her feet on the toilet and I casually exited the stall. I looked at the VERY pissed off

NASCAR lovin' redneck and said: "Dude, you do NOT want to go in there!" Looking very much intent on murder he grunted and left the bathroom. Nine lives???? Me??? Try INFINITY bitches! Now back to the double delight.

My crazy ass-freak girlfriend and I were partying at the club. We had pre-gamed with a little of the **finest plant every produced by nature**, and in my belief the plant that could bring about world peace. A couple of drinks into the night, things were going as I would have expected. We were having fun joking with friends and making fun of the posers in the bar. I also got to sit in with the band for a couple of songs. My girl excused herself to run to the ladies room and I hung out on a bar stool taking a break from the action. It turned out that this was the calm before what would turn into a **"Sex Tsunami."**

When my girlfriend came back to the bar, a girl was with her that I knew from playing the bar scene. I never thought the two knew each other, but apparently they knew each other well enough to strike up a conversation in the bathroom. Susan looked me in the eye and said: "Gregg, Erin would

like to fuck us". No need to ask for clarification on that statement! I *am* suspicious of bullshit by nature so I played it cool. Without any sense of shock on my face I deadpanned: "Yeah, good one". Erin then spoke up and said: "I haven't tried a three-way before Gregg, but we were talking about it and it sounds like fun!" I mentally did a quick verification that I had ONLY smoked **weed** before we went out and did not ingest any hardcore hallucinogens! I have never tripped in my life. Control issues. Any substance where you need someone to babysit you scares the shit out of me! I made the slightest hint at again calling bullshit when they turned to each other and started their tongues dancing AND grabbing at each other's tits! HOLY FUCK!

People around the bar were starting to take notice. This was NOT BULLSHIT after all! Check please!!! I wanted to quickly move **this** party to a more private location. Susan insisted on riding with Erin and that I follow them back to Erin's place. As I was starting my car, I watched the two of them furiously making out in Erin's car while waiting for me to get rolling. When we got back to

Erin's place, what is now a fond surreal memory began.

Straight to the bedroom, no tours of the house and no detours! They wanted total control of the order of events and I was more than happy to comply. I got to freelance a little once things got rolling but hey, whatever it takes to get the party started!

Susan and Erin teamed up to make short order of getting my clothes off. They pushed me onto the bed and ordered me to just watch for a while. **Can you really "order" the completely willing and horny??** Anyway…….these two picked up where they left off at the bar. This was way too cool. It was like watching live porn WITHOUT being left alone to jerk off at the end!

They made out furiously while peeling off each other's clothes. After feeling up each other for a bit, they dropped onto the bed to start taking care of Gregg Beerpussy's South Pole. Susan started doing her usual expert knob-schlob while Erin stared with a wickedly yearning look on her face. She interrupted Susan asking: "Susan PLEASE, would it be ok if I sucked his dick?" My

brain……racing……**please say yes**, please fucking say **YES**!!!…..holding my breath here!!!! Helloooooo!!!! Susan pointed my cock in Erin's direction like a scepter and said "Go for it!" WHY THE FUCK DIDN'T I MARRY THIS GIRL?? Oh yeah, the psycho part. *sigh* Erin eagerly took her turn pleasing a VERY happy Mr. Beerpussy. She and Susan took turns switching back and forth which nearly sent me over the edge WAY too early. I am sure the alcohol actually HELPED in this instance. No worries, if that happened I am sure I could have **once again** risen to the occasion. This was a night of infinite boners!

 I was rockin' like a porn star. It was time for Gregg Beerpussy to take charge. I rocked them while they were side by side, double decker or one on the other's face while I was doing my thing! I made sure that if I had seen it done, or imagined doing it…….it got done dammit! NEVER WASTE THIS KIND OF OPPORTUNITY!! Hitting you with some Beerpussy knowledge… more valuable than college bitches!

The only unfortunate thing about this whole experience is that it happened on a week night and

my nine to five bank job was approaching quickly. Ok, I take that back. Fuck it. There is nothing negative in this situation! A lot of guys would give up one of their gonads for what I got that night! I am grateful and will shut the fuck up. LOL

I took a quick snooze, and then woke up to massively consume the strongest coffee I could find. It was so strong that it was borderline meth. This is one of those times you wake up and you feel like that horse stomped on your head and fucked you in the eye! Damn Susan got to stay up all night having sex and then sleep in. I had a three-way. Sleep in my dear……as much….. as you FUCKING WANT!

I saw a call coming through from Susan on my work phone a little later in the morning. She sounded a *little weird* on the other end, so I pressed. She said "Um…….I was *wondering* if last night made you feel *any* differently about me." Wow." NOOO! Of course not!" Ha, silly girl! "If anything, it makes me feel great about you. You are SO unselfish. Thank you soooooo much honey!"

 Damn I'm good. Smooth but not overboard. I said exactly what needed to be said. "I am so happy to hear you so that!" Using the superhero status I had just achieved and being the sexual opportunistic bastard I am, I decided to ask if we could ever play with Erin again. She said she would be willing AND she asked if the two of them could have some occasional one on one time. Of course you can! Go for it. Why was I so open-minded and willing to let them go solo???? They also liked to take pictures ;) Click click click and up went my dick! My very own "Girls on Film" Long live Duran Duran! If it wasn't for Duran Duran, I would have never worn eyeliner on stage…………AND convince my father I MUST be gay in the process ☺

Not sure why, but I never felt like a girlfriend would be cheating if she got it on with another chick. Girls seem to naturally have much more intimate emotional relationships with each other anyway.

 If it is to each other that they bitch and whine, then why not let them 69? ☺

Cucumbers and Vampires

"Pain is temporary but virginity wasn't going to last forever!"–Gregg B.

Sid Beerpussy created more demented stories than I can possibly remember. The most extreme shit is what burns in my brain like an unrelenting herpes sore. The fact that ANY of us sick motherfuckers aren't dead, in jail or rehab is nothing short of a Goddamn miracle! We all had our twisted side but NONE of us were in Sid's league. He took things to a whole new level.

One night I remember hooking up with some punker chicks either at a bar or house party. Alcohol haze has obscured some details but I ended up having a romp with one of them. As I was about to hit full throttle and go balls deep she said: "Wait! I am a virgin so I need you to go slowly. Is that ok?" IS IT OK??? REALLY?? You bet your intact hymen it is! Gregg Beerpussy no

more! I am now Buster…..Buster Hymen. Normally I might recoil a bit at the prospect of de-virginizing a girl I did not intend on dating. Yes, I did have **some** standards. I guess I just always thought that most girls would want to lose their virginity to a guy they were dating or whatever. Well, this was apparently NOT one of those girls! She was on a quest to let me penetrate her pleasure chest. We did the deed, she THANKED me and that was pretty much it. My dear, you are welcome! I actually felt honored to have her totally use me to accomplish her goal.

This young lady was **definitely** on a mission to explore her wild side. She moved on from a one night stand with me to a semi-regular thing with Sid! This switch up was **totally** cool. She and I were a no-strings one night stand. Sid dug her and she was into the whole punker thing, so it was a match.

 The situation for Sid was perfect! She was open to experimentation and he was a MAD SCIENTIST! Dr. Brown-Eye, AA (All Anal). ALL of us were guilty of this to a degree, but Sid especially liked

to see just HOW dirty he could get a girl to be. They didn't call him "Dr. Brown-Eye" for nothing.

With his enthusiastic subject he engaged in frequent experimentation. Things started with the not-so-crazy and eventually went to a level that……ooops, almost gave away the ending. I hate when I finish too soon! Wait a sec……dammit!! Clean up on aisle five! Ok, all cleaned up and a fresh set of boxers. Read on….

When I opened this girl's velvet love tunnel for business, I apparently unleashed a **highly orgasmic** sex fiend. Sid was having a blast! YOU ARE WELCOME YOU DEMENTED BASTARD! Eventually the standard blow job, crotch munching and humping and pumping got a *little* boring.

Sid decided to get creative and put his green thumb and artistic talents to use. He told her to wait in the bedroom while he went to the kitchen. Sid pulled a cucumber from the refrigerator and set about carving a perfectly shaped vegetarian schlong! The man is a **fucking artist**. Just to be clear, the cucumber was certified organic, no GMO's and

pesticide free! When he returned to the bedroom she was laughing hysterically BUT did not shy away from trying out the garden-fresh dong. Sid started working the green phallus in and out and the excitement of trying something different REALLY got her going. Then things went a little south............south of the border.

Sid's highly orgasmic subject started to climax SO HARD that her fun box severed the cucumber like a pussy guillotine! I guess you could say they were in a pickle. Hmmm.....I guess after enough time it could literally pickle???? That would be a barrel of laughs. Would it be dill or sweet?? These are the questions that come to the mind of a **twisted fuck** like me! No apologies for the bad puns. Fuck you all. Anyway.....the way the story was relayed to me, the problem was solved with her bearing down and Sid performing a game of "Operation" with a pair of tongs. The procedure was a success! They gave "Tossing the salad" a whole new meaning.

 I guess the lesson learned here is that a cucumber can work as a sex toy but DAMMIT, leave the skin on! No wonder it broke! I am sure the cucumber cock was one fucking fantastic work of art. It

should have been preserved and put on display in some fucked up museum.

I mentioned several times that Sid likes to push the limits and take things *a bit over the edge*. After the last story some of you might wonder HOW MUCH more over the edge he could go! Sit right back and you'll hear a tale, a tale of a fateful trip……….that started on a small mattress and ended with some drips. Don't worry, that will make sense in a minute. If you don't remember Gilligan's Island, the reference will never make sense! History lesson: Never forget that EVERY guy wanted to do Mary Ann WAY more than Ginger. There was something about Mary Ann that just screamed she would fuck you silly. Yep, jerked off to that thought too! What HAVEN'T I jerked off too???? **That** will require some reflection……

Sid was horny as usual, and decided to pay his veggie-snapper girlfriend a surprise daytime visit. She was half asleep in her bed, so Sid crawled in next to her and innocently cuddled for a while. He decided that cuddle time was over and it was time to go head long into a muff dive.

It took her a second to realize his what he was up to. When she realized what was about to happen she yelled "NOOOO, OH MY FUCKING GOD I'M ON THE RAG!!!" YOU DON"T WANT TO DO THAT!" Sid curiously studied the tail of the white tail rat hanging from Aunt Flo's house. Sid growled, snarled like a rabid dog, then grabbed the string with his teeth and YANKED Dracula's tea bag from its box like it was a raw hide chew toy! He then came up with what now looked like a red clown face as he whipped the dripping womb-wick side to side from his clenched teeth like a proud beast!

I asked Sid at one point how things were going with her. He told me that it was over. Apparently he found that her limit was bloody vampire tampon wagging! She was SO freaked out that she started screaming at him to leave. Oh well, I guess they weren't a match after all, especially blood type! She wanted the "Big O", just not O-positive.

I guess she liked me more

"Dude, you did WHAT!? But I liked her!"- Friends of Gregg Beerpussy

ALL of the women we met were fair game as far as I was concerned. If no one spoke up about their feelings for a girl, how was I to know if they were "digging" her or trying to work on a relationship? Communication is the key! Besides, if she was REALLY into you, she wouldn't be looking at anyone else. That is of course for a select few girls who just had the goal of fucking everyone in, or associated with, the band. There were at least a few of those.

 More than once a conversation would start with one of us bragging about getting a blow job in a club bathroom and then another would speak up about banging the **same** girl in the band truck

between sets the week before! There were a couple of occasions where I, the purveyor of poonany that I was, upset some of my bandmates by having a flesh fiesta with a senorita they had their eye on.

A trio of young ladies affectionately known as "The Baltimore Girls" followed the band around that I used to run sound for. These guys were your basic cover band. This part of rock n' roll will always amaze me. Even an average cover band can attract a following that is willing to drive over an hour just to hang out with you!

Of these three particular girls, one possessed the look of a young Kim Bassinger, with her full lips and long blond hair. She was soft spoken and seemed VERY shy. The second was a pretty Jewish girl with jet black hair and a nice bubble ass. The third………well….let's just say you wouldn't have banged her at three am after several shots of tequila. I am being nice! I call that "Wolf Pussy". Pussy so nasty it will snarl back at you and howl at the moon. She is probably listed on WebMD as the cure for a boner. The thought of attempting a hat-trick with this crew was out of the question.

I have always found Jewish women in general very attractive and this one was outgoing so it was easy to work the Beerpussy magic. I spun her kosher twat like a dradle around the mattress. Cock meat is apparently NOT on the Hebrew list of forbidden foods! Alas that relationship was short-lived.

She surprised me by showing up at a house party we were playing. I happened to be upstairs between sets helping a young lady learn to sing from her diaphragm. Of course I had to show her how to loosen up her vocal chords first ;) So……….no more Jewish American Princess.

 I was a little bit bummed even though I was not *technically* in a relationship with her. I liked using my dick, not *feeling* like one. I was certain the "Baltimore Girls" would not be coming to any more gigs.

It turns out that I must have thought a little too much of myself because they continued to show up! My Hebrew honey was now trying to go after another member of the band in what I can only assume was an attempt to make me jealous. Whatever! The next adventure caught me off

guard, but luckily I am a quick thinker and took full advantage of the situation. Beerpussy lighting was about to strike yet again. Time to rock like a hurricane. Long live the Scorpions!

The Kim Bassinger look-alike, the hottest of the three, was sitting next to me at a table between sets. Everyone else was also hanging out nearby. We were making small talk when **out of nowhere** she leaned in closely and with her lips nearly touching my ear whispered : " Do you ever feel sometimes like you just want a piece of ass?". What an insanely lucky bastard I am. With that I looked at her with a smile and said: "Why yes! Matter of fact….. NOW happens to be one of those times!" With an arm around her waist, I slung her over my shoulder like a horny cave-man going in search of a place to fuck her back to the stone-age. Strike while it's hot…..I am an unashamed ass opportunist!

The club had a kitchen that was not in use and I decided the "special" on the menu that night was going to be pink snapper surprise. We went into the pantry and in no time pants were off and I was standing up taking her from behind as she knocked

canned foods off the shelf in an orgasmic rage. Repeat after me: "Gregg is God!!!"

Eventually she started shouting "COME DAMMIT! COME NOW! I WANT TO MAKE YOU COME!!!" So much for shy and reserved! I came SO FUCKING HARD that I am sure I left "special sauce" behind for the cook to use the next day. Things then became even more surreal.

She kept kissing and stroking my face while asking me if she pleased me and IF SHE WAS GOOD ENOUGH!!!! I should have immediately proposed marriage but…………you usually don't end up marrying the person who had sex with you for the first time in the pantry of a dive bar! Usually.

As we were loading out our gear that night the drummer said: "Gregg, I saw you carrying one of the Baltimore girls to the back of the club. What was up with that?????" I recounted our **porno fuck scene** and watched his face as it went from a blank expression, to sadness and then anger. He then yelled, "DAMMIT GREGG, I LIKED HER!!!" Oh well, I guess she liked me more!

From playing around our small local scene there were times you weren't even PLAYING a club but would wind up getting laid BECAUSE girls recognized you. It was like picking low hanging fruit at times. Just too damn easy! These adventures were usually fun because the girls were downright bold and there was no mistaking what intentions were or guesswork as to how the night would end.

One night I met a girl who actually wore me out to the point where I had to throw her out of my apartment! I am ashamed to admit it, but there was no head left on THIS Beerpussy. Another issue is that she also let out this extremely loud groan when she came that sounded like a farm animal being slaughtered! It could be heard through a few blocks of the college town where I lived. I could hear the muffled laughter and yells of "WHAT THE FUCK IS THAT!!?" each time she reached the pleasure zone. It was like I was running a pussy slaughter house!

I was never afraid to go into a bar alone on a pussy recon mission. A Navy Seal of socializing I was. Due to my outgoing nature, I always seemed to

end up with a few new friends wherever I went and was a magnet for crazy shit.

Whenever I was out I would usually run into other musicians that were out partying or showing support for a friend's band. Like me, they were sometimes out for the hell of it…….just looking for a good time.

I ran into a bass player from another band who was a smug prick. He was sitting at a table next to a pretty girl and flashed me a smirk of superiority. Little did he know that his eye candy was already a fan of a good Beerpussy banging! Ha ha….fuckin' ha!!!! Dick.

 I sat down across from her and started talking to them and I could see her face getting flushed and I swear she had a look that said she was getting aroused. My Beerpussy senses were dead on accurate. While I was talking to the smug prick bass player, I felt her foot sliding up my leg and RIGHT ONTO MY COCK! Good thing I have an awesome poker face. It was obvious by the way she kept at it that she had done this before and was NOT going to stop until I popped. Shouting to

make it look like I was impressed by the band, I blew my load right there under the table after I could not handle her magic foot anymore! This girl had skills. The smug prick dude got up to hit the bathroom and when he was out of sight she started laughing her ass off as she wrote down her phone number! We did meet up a couple weeks later for a night of no holds barred fun. So…..HEY….Smug prick……I guess she liked me more ☺

One particular night I was hanging out in a local tavern where we played on a couple of occasions. Looking every bit the eighties rock n' roller that I was, I leaned up against a wall when I noticed a couple of girls staring at me and giggling. Was my zipper down???? Did I not look as cool as I thought???? No, that couldn't possibly be the case! I flashed a smile and put my hands out as if to ask what the fuck they were laughing about! Just then, one of them stared into my eyes and gave me the "Come hither" signal to join her at the table.

 The summoning vixen said she knew of my band and had seen us play there before. I appreciate directness and this moment definitely made me smile when she said:" I was telling my girlfriend

here how much fun I would have fucking you!" Me:" Um, so………… do you live around here?" You can never let the Beerpussy go stale!

Back at her place we were going to town before every piece of clothing could fly off of our bodies. Standing…sitting…..the floor and then to doggy style on the couch…you name it! In the midst of this maniacal fuck fest I committed the classic sex foul MOST woman dread: slipping out of hole #1 and plunging full force into hole #2 which results in a condition known as "Anus Complainus".This accidental plunge into her turd cutter was met with a reaction I DID NOT expect. Instead of screaming and pulling away she kept panting and said:" Oh my God, you and Sid!!!" Huh, WHAT??? "Me and Sid what?????" I asked while I continued the unexpected foray into her fart flume. She said: "Your bass player, he likes to stick it in my ass too!" HO…..HO….HOLY SHIT! I wanted to bust out laughing but hey, I have class.

Sid and I were hanging out the next day and I told him about the girl I hooked up with and what went down. At first he laughed but then he asked where she lived. I told him the neighborhood and he said:

"Oh man, that's Stacy!" I said:" Yeah, so?" Then he replied with a statement I was getting TOO used to hearing: "DAMMIT GREGG, I LIKED HER!!!"

Oh well, I guess she liked me more ☺

MILF: Mick and I are Lucky Fuckers

"That which doesn't make you stronger just hurts like bloody hell!"- My friend Dave

As I mentioned in the introduction, Mick and I were masters of MILF before the term was coined. Married moms who were out frequently at bars seemed to really like the appeal of young men that were anxious to get in their pants. That is the kind of shit that happens when husbands neglect their wives! Or……marry sluts.

At that time of our lives I confess that Mick and I did not have many morals OR were too horny to care about being down with OPP. That stands for Other People's Pussy for those of you too young to remember. Long live Naughty by Nature! The next two tales of banging some "Broken-in baby makers" had the potential to end badly, so they

definitely stick out in my mind. There could be more stories, but again those brain cells are dead or the memories are repressed and will come out in therapy!

As I have said before: If you are not playing in the band, the next best job is being the sound or light man. You are visible to all the people in the club, have a great view of the crowd and have the most access to girls on the prowl. In my experience, if they can't fuck a guy in the band, the soundman gets to eat……sorry….pick… the low hanging fruit!

One night I was running sound at a club where the soundboard was perfectly positioned on a riser near the entrance. I could see who was walking in and scope out the talent. The sound check was complete so to occupy my time before the band started, I was periodically checking the talent walking in. I had worked this club more than once and it was RIPE with girls looking for a good time.

The club was far enough into redneck country that it was the only entertainment for miles so the people coming in were ready to party. I spied a

cute girl coming in alone and motioned to the doorman to not charge a cover and told him that she was with the band. She gave me a smile and nod that I will never forget. Little did I know at the time that the smile was the start of what was a fun but equally FUCKED UP NIGHT!!

While I was working, a waitress showed up with a shot of liquor. She said someone wanted to buy me a round and motioned in the direction of the bar where that same girl smiled, waved and we downed our shots at the same time. By the second set, she was sitting next to me at the soundboard. Third set, she was stroking my rock hard **vagina viper** underneath the table!

Our conversation moved to the parking lot and here is where I dropped one of the CHEESIEST lines which fortunately was overlooked. I said "Hey, ummm…why don't we sit in your car to….uhhhhh….talk?" Yes…..drunk, horny AND stupid I was! She looked at me and deadpanned: "I am a married woman, you know what I want. Follow me." GAME ON! I followed this girl at high rates of speed on some of the worst bum-fuck

country back roads imaginable all the way to………..………..HER TRAILER PARK!

 I would have fucked this girl in a dumpster at this point so, what the fuck. Things continued to get weird, but again, too drunk to care. It was then that I found out that her brother and his wife were there! WTF??? They seemed to have no issues at all with this girl bringing a strange guy home. Guess that's the way things are in them thar parts!

After the kinfolk left she told me to sit on the couch and relax. In a few minutes she came out of the bedroom wearing some of the finest Kmart lingerie money could buy and motioned me toward the bedroom in her double-wide. This girl was so pent up that I was in pain for days, everywhere from my dick to my face! She rode my mouth so hard I had the pussy eating version of road rash. I could have sworn I was going to either lose teeth (to match her relatives) or bust my lip!

 I slammed as hard as she ordered and my only slip was the accidental surprise of a quick dick sneak in her ass. Seems to happen a lot with me, huh? Hey, it was dark, my aim was bad and after the pain she

was inflicting on me, I didn't feel that badly about it! I just made a course correction and kept drilling like I was pumping for oil to send her, Jethro and Grandpa packing up and moving to Beverly………Hills that is…..swimming pools….movie stars.

Once we were finished doing the trailer park tango, mobile home mombo, or whatever, we both passed out……COMPLETELY spent. When I woke up in the morning things got even more fucked up. The noise that woke me was the sound of her fucking kids!! She got them to go back to their rooms so that I could get dressed and leave. I asked her if they saw me and she said: "Yeah, but since you have long hair I just told them it was their aunt". Ha! THAT was funny!

 What was not funny was the sight of the rifle case next to the bed. SHIT! It was then that I envisioned her husband coming home and filling us both full of buckshot! I quickly put on my clothes and made my exit from her corn-hole and dashed through the cornfields!

My pussy rash face and I made it safely home, into the shower and then back to bed for recovery just thankful not to be nursing any gunshot wounds.

Mick Beerpussy is one of the luckiest motherfuckers on the planet. I was dating a girl named Sharon. She had a friend named Karen and the two were inseparable. They would show up to every gig together and dance with each other the entire night. Sharon was separated from her husband but Karen was still VERY MUCH married and her spouse was away periodically for days at a time. That was a relationship ripe for disaster.

Sharon and I started dating and had an awesome sexual relationship. In hindsight it is pretty amazing that she actually made me hold out for a while before giving up the prize! One night we arranged to meet at a hotel and the sex hit Mach 1. We did it until it hurt. Seems to be another pattern with me, huh? We went at it so many times that instead of coming, I would hear a puff of air. I had NOTHING left to give! I eventually started to realize that she was WAY more experimental than I originally thought.

Every now and then Mick and I would make a trip to Karen's apartment to meet up with the two of them to just hang out and party a little. Things changed one night when we added a little of Jamaica's finest export to the mix.

Mick and I found ourselves in the bedroom with Karen while Sharon was chilling and completely zoned out in front of the TV. Things then started to get fun. Sharon was making out with Mick while I was running my hands all over her body. I briefly took a break to clue Sharon in on the activities. With a devilish smile crossing her face, she came in to observe the action.

While I worked off Karen's pants, Sharon was getting horny as hell and quickly stripped out of her clothing. She watched as I went down on her friend until she came so hard that she screamed loudly enough to scare the neighbors! I moved over to Sharon and started to work over her already dripping pussy.

We both stole glances at Mick and Karen as Mick relentlessly pounded her in what was an epic display by both of them. Kudos, my friends! Mick

then moved over to assist in my quest to please Sharon. What a friend! Here is where one of the most classic lines was uttered that is still brought up and laughed about hysterically until this day.

I slid up to drop my flesh popsicle into Sharon's mouth so that Mick could go down on her. This went on for a bit until Mick spoke up and uttered his famous request: "Gregg, would you mind moving up a bit? I REALLY DON'T LIKE LOOKING AT YOUR ASSHOLE WHILE I EAT YOUR GIRLFRIENDS PUSSY!!"

At the time I was not sure what was funnier: the question itself or the sound of Sharon's gargling laugh with my manhood in her mouth!!!!So, being the nice guy I am………I slid up! I remember the laughter all the way home and Mick slamming the wheel of his car while laughing and saying: "HOLY SHIT!!! WE JUST BANGED TWO MARRIED MOM'S!!! WHAT THE FUCK????!!!" Our pride was almost destroyed by what turned out to be one of the most surreal experiences I have EVER been a part of.

Mick and I were working sound and lights for a band that was playing in the town where Sharon and Karen lived. As I was standing near the soundboard with Mick, I noticed Karen and her husband out of the corner of my eye AND they were making their way in our direction. OHHHHHHHH FUCK! I was ready for a blood bath. No matter what, I would back up Mick in ANY situation and was **convinced** some major shit was about to go down. They both approached and in a very civil manner, Karen said to Mick: "Joe (her husband) has something to tell you". Joe reached out to shake Mick's hand and said: "You're cool man. I knew she was going to cheat on me eventually and at least I am glad it was you". WTF????!!!Are you fucking kidding me??? Mick banged a MARRIED MOM and the husband thanked him for it???!!! I was part of the action too, but I guess that part was left out of her story. In a sick way I wanted to speak up and say: "Well I made her come, will you buy me a drink too??" LOL. Mick, the lucky motherfucker.

Don't mess with Mr. Beerpussy

Tommy Nuttbutter

"Revenge is sweet, but sometimes salty"

- Gregg Beerpussy

There is ONE in every band. Tommy was that one "member" who came across as one of the guys, but in reality he was a total douche. Awesome drummer, but a REAL DICK.

Tommy would do things like short everyone's pay at the end of a gig so that he could score a case of beer from the bar owner. He would talk about you behind your back to girls you were banging so that HE could score a piece of ass. Instead of getting his pussy the old fashioned way (earning it) he would try to scam yours. Things weren't always that way. Tommy could attract his share of pussy. There was one girl he turned me on to named

Shelly. Tommy started off by sharing prized flesh just like the rest of us.

I'll never forget the first night he introduced me to Shelly. Tommy had a scooter and he was taking Shelly for a ride to a friend of ours so we could shoot some pool. Little did I know, Tommy was talking Shelly into a stop at a dark local softball field! To say Shelly was a nymphomaniac is an understatement.

 I found out later that she immediately knew what was up. She asked Tommy "We are going for a three way aren't we?" Tommy just replied: "You cool with that???" Of course she was! Out on the softball field that night she took more balls off her mound than a major league catcher. Tommy and I unleashed our Louisville Sluggers and only stopped scoring due to the mercy rule!

Throughout the next couple of years I had many run-ins with Shelly apart from Tommy. There were some fun times like when Shelly started experimenting with other chicks and they would gladly put on lesbo shows for us. She also could give blowjobs legends are made of. That girl could

suck so hard you would need to pull the bed sheets out of your ass!

One session involving Shelly and I started at a restaurant and ended with us meeting up at my apartment with a waitress and bartender for a late night four-way free for all. I was definitely partying like a rock star!

Shelly was blowing me on the couch, I banged the waitress on the couch, the bartender and waitress went at it on the stairs and there was the grand finale of Shelly and I pulling a shower-to-bathroom-sink romp. Maybe it was at this point Tommy started getting a little jealous?? Just guessing. Who knows, WHO FUCKING CARES??!!!

Things definitely took a turn when I started dating another little nympho whose name I truly don't remember. I will call her Shit-Twat. Being my generous self and returning the Shelly favor, I let Tommy join me in a session of pleasing Shit-Twat. It was here that the severe backstabbing started.

Shelly was NEVER Tommy's girlfriend. I broke no rules. Shit-twat was *technically* my girlfriend.

Even though we all sometimes shared, there was an understanding that sharing did not mean ongoing permission to SHAG SOMEONE'S GIRLFRIEND! Band code! After I was spent for the night, Tommy and Shit-Twat hung out in the corner of the room talking. I could overhear Tommy telling her that I was just using her and that he really liked her and I was banging other girls…..on and on…blah blah blah. That is when he became a douchebag! That greedy motherfucker. Revenge mode, activate!

I am COMPLETELY amazed but maybe I should be flattered that Tommy wanted my sloppy seconds. He actually went on and got engaged to her! Fucking loser. Big surprise….it didn't last. Maybe Gregg Beerpussy had set the bar too high??? Who am I to brag? I never cared about the two of them shacking up. More power to them. It was the breaking of guy code that got under my skin.

Here is some BEERPUSSY WISDOM (ladies especially take note): If the ONLY way a guy can try to score is by PUTTING DOWN the guy that a girl is spending time with, he is a LOSER! What

this type of guy is saying is that he has NOTHING to offer. Because he is a loser, he will attempt to make another dude look BAD in order to get laid. AMATUERS! They need to get some "game" of their own and not try to steal from those of us who have it! On the other hand, if a girl is gullible enough to fall for that rap, she wasn't worth having around in the first place. And now "COMES" the revenge. LITERALLY.

So…………It was a random night hanging out at the band house. A little bit of rehearsing was going on and even more goofing off. Things were SO crazy in the house that hearing random moaning and screaming coming from any room was normal. You never knew if it was someone working on a new tune or working over a willing guest.

 Shelly and I were messing around on the couch while Tommy was downstairs working on some drum parts. As I mentioned before, Shelly could suck the flesh popsicle (scepter of love, bayonet, schlong, schween, Loch Ness Monster) like a pro! While Shelly was touching my schlong to her vocal chords, the drummer from another band casually walked in and without batting an eye,

walked through the living room where we were. As he walked by he just gave a casual wave and a "Hey guys, things good?" I gave a smile and nod while Shelly gave a gurgled and slightly muffled laugh. Nothing out of the ordinary in THIS house! What happened next was Gregg Beerpussy's revenge on Tommy Nuttbutter.

Shelly stopped her oral magic to get on all fours so that I could go Atomic Dog Style. Bow wow wow yippee yo yippee yay! Long live P-Funk!!! On a side note……. Have any guys out there done it rodeo style? That is when you are doing your girl from behind and say:" Your sister (or friend) likes it this way too" and then you try to hold on for three seconds! Ride 'em cowboy!!! But I digress………

 Tommy came upstairs, looked at us and said "Don't come inside her Gregg, I want to go down on her later." What???? ARE YOU FUCKING SERIOUS????!!! This SICK FUCK was going to lick her love tunnel after I had been giving it a legendary Beerpussy work out! While Shelly was an eager beaver, from the look on her face I don't think she liked being talked about like property.

She simply liked to fuck and was not ashamed. Nothing wrong with that at all.

BEERPUSSY WISDOM: It is a travesty that if a guy bangs a lot of girls he is a stud, but if a girl bangs a lot of guys….she is a slut. WRONG! Get over it. If a girl wants to go out and get a random piece of ass, don't judge! Why should a girl be required to just sit at home with a battery operated boyfriend? Unless of course most guys she knows are assholes and doesn't want the hassle! LOL

After Tommy walked out, Shelly and I switched to missionary and continued our insanely fun recreational pounding. As we were both about to come Shelly and I both had wicked smiles cross our faces. Breathless I asked: "are you thinking what I am thinking?" She moaned "YES, DON'T…. PULL…. OUT!!!!" Laughing like a mad hyena I emptied every last drop of love juice into Shelly's come catching muffin.

Later that night Shelly called me hysterically laughing as she described Tommy going down on her later that night! Somehow she had to mask her laughter during Tommy's crotch munching,

ESPECIALLY when Tommy commented on how wet she was! OH YES, REVENGE IS SWEET TOMMY…AND SOMETIMES SALTY!!

THAT'S RIGHT ASSHOLE!! You lapped up my love seed, my man jam, my pecker snot, my nut butter, my slimy semen surprise. FUCK YOU DOUCHEBAG! Repeat again my children: GREGG BEERPUSSY IS GOD…..LONG LIVE GREGG BEERPUSSY!

<u>Final Thoughts</u>

I never regret any of the girls that I had sex with - <u>*I only regret the ones I didn't!*</u>

I was always an, <u>*"eager to please lover."*</u> My goal is to have a girl not just brag about having sex with me - I wanted her to brag about how **<u>GOOD</u>** it was! (No, I was not ALWAYS successful…but I strive for constant improvement!)

She might just be serious about wanting that three-way…**<u>YOU NEVER KNOW!</u>**

Anal sex should <u>*NOT*</u> set a girl on fire!

Never search for your bag of weed when you are stoned. Matter of fact; do not search for ANYTHING when you are stoned: It is a fruitless endeavor.

Do not trust a girl's intelligence who says: "You won't catch herpes if you stick it in my ass."

Do not assume that I, Gregg Beerpussy, Lord of Lords, did NOT blow my load before leaving her tuna tunnel.

TELL ME YOU LIKE HER BEFORE I ASS BANG HER!!!!

<u>TELL ME</u> you like her before I do her caveman style in a restaurant pantry. Please????

It is really hard not to freak out when you go back to a girl's place at night and realize during sex that there is a baby in the room.

I do not mind moving up while you eat my girlfriend's pussy. It is the least I can do.

Those shotguns on the wall??? He never uses them**… right??????**

Most girls who dig *<u>A LOT</u>* of anal are a little psycho.

Bathroom stalls can be a dangerous place to get a blowjob, <u>especially</u> when the husband comes looking for her.

Learn to actually play your instrument; *__you have already mastered your skin flute!__*

__Grab a tissue…..I think you have some Beerpussy on your lips!__

VIVA LA BEERPUSSY!!

www.ingramcontent.com/pod-product-compliance
Lightning Source LLC
LaVergne TN
LVHW021400080426
835508LV00020B/2373